ARACHNID W RLD
FISHINGSPIDERS

SANDRA MARKLE

WATER NINJAS

↳ LERNER PUBLICATIONS COMPANY MINNEAPOLIS

FOR CURIOUS KIDS EVERYWHERE

ACKNOWLEDGMENTS

The author would like to thank Dr. Robert B. Suter, Vassar College, Poughkeepsie, New York, and Dr. Simon Pollard, Canterbury Museum, Christchurch, New Zealand, for sharing their expertise and enthusiasm. A special thanks to Skip Jeffery for his support during the creation of this book.

Lerner Publications Company
A division of Lerner Publishing Group, Inc.
241 First Avenue North
Minneapolis, MN 55401 U.S.A.

Website address: www.lernerbooks.com

Library of Congress Cataloging-in-Publication Data

Markle, Sandra.
    Fishing spiders : water ninjas / by Sandra Markle.
        p.   cm. — (Arachnid world)
    Includes bibliographical references and index.
    ISBN 978–0–7613–5044–6 (lib. bdg. : alk. paper)
    1. Dolomedes—Juvenile literature. I. Title.
    QL458.42.P5M35 2012
    595.4′4—dc23   2011020442

Manufactured in the United States of America
1 – DP – 12/31/11

CONTENTS

AN ARACHNID'S WORLD

WELCOME TO THE WORLD OF ARACHNIDS

(ah-RACK-nidz). Arachnids can be found in every habitat on Earth except in the deep ocean.

So how can you tell if an animal is an arachnid rather than a relative like the insect shown below? Both belong to a group of animals called arthropods (AR-throh-podz). The animals in this group share some traits. They have bodies divided into segments, jointed legs, and a stiff exoskeleton. This is a skeleton on the outside like a suit of armor. But one way that usually works to tell if an animal is an arachnid is to count its

legs and body parts. While not every adult arachnid has eight legs, most do. Arachnids also usually have two main body parts. Most adult insects, like this diving beetle *(right)*, have six legs and three main body parts.

This book is about a group of spiders called *Dolomedes* (doh-loh-MEE-deez). These arachnids are sneaky water ninjas, especially adapted to catching prey (living things to eat) from the water's surface *(facing page)*.

A fishing spider's body temperature rises and falls with the temperature around it. It must warm up to be active.

OUTSIDE AND INSIDE

ON THE OUTSIDE

There are about one hundred different kinds of fishing spiders. Like this great raft spider, they all share certain features. They all have two main body parts: the cephalothorax (sef-uh-loh-THOR-ax) and the abdomen. A waistlike part called the pedicel joins the two. The spider's exoskeleton is made up of many plates. Stretchy tissue connects the plates so the spider can bend and move.

Take a close look at the outside of this female fishing spider to discover other key features all fishing spiders share.

SPINNERETS:
These parts
shoot out the
spider's silk.

LEGS:
These are used
for walking, climbing,
and rowing or for
galloping across the
water's surface.

PEDICEL

ABDOMEN

CEPHALOTHORAX

PEDIPALPS: These are a pair of leglike parts that extend from the head near the mouth. They help catch prey and hold it for eating. In males the pedipalps are also used during reproduction.

CHELICERAE (keh-LIH-seh-ree): This is a pair of strong, jawlike parts near the mouth. They have a sawlike edge that can crush and tear and end in fangs that can inject venom (liquid poison).

EYES: These sensory organs detect light and send messages to the brain for sight. Fishing spiders usually have eight eyes.

ON THE INSIDE

Look inside an adult female dark fishing spider.

VENOM GLAND: This body part produces venom.

BRAIN: This part sends and receives messages to and from all other body parts.

PHARYNX (FAR-inks): This muscular tube pumps food into the stomach. Hairs in it help filter out any solid waste.

TRACHEAE (TRAY-kee-ee): These tubes let air enter through holes called spiracles. Tracheae spread oxygen throughout the spider's body.

NERVE GANGLIA: These bundles of nerve tissue send messages between the brain and other body parts.

CAECA (SEE-kuh): These branching tubes pass food nutrients into the blood. They also store food.

COXAL (KAHK-sel) GLANDS: These special groups of cells collect liquid wastes and pass them through openings to the outside.

Approved by Dr. Simon Pollard, Canterbury Museum, Christchurch, New Zealand

SUCKING STOMACH: This stomach works with the pharynx to move food between the mouth and the gut. Cells in the lining produce digestive fluids.

HEART: This muscular tube pumps blood toward the head. Then the blood flows back to the heart.

MALPHIGHIAN (mal-PIG-ee-an) TUBULES: This system of tube cleans the bloo of wastes.

GUT: This tube lets food nutrients pass into the blood.

STERCORAL (STER-kor-ul) POCKET: The body part where wastes collect before passing out of the body.

OVA This part pro egg

SILK GLAND: This body part produces silk.

BOOK LUNGS: These are thin, flat folds of tissue. Oxygen from the air passes through them and enters the spider's blood. Waste carbon dioxide gas exits through them.

GONOPORE: This is the reproductive opening.

SPERMATHECA (spur-muh-THEE-kuh): This sac stores sperm after mating.

BECOMING ADULTS

Like all arachnids, fishing spiders go through incomplete metamorphosis (meh-tuh-MOHR-fuh-sus). *Metamorphosis* means "change." A fishing spider's life includes three stages: egg, nymph or spiderling, and adult.

Spiderlings hatch from their eggs inside an egg sac. At first, they are blind and unable to eat. They stay in the egg sac for a few days until they molt, or shed their

SOME KINDS OF ARTHROPODS, SUCH AS INSECTS, GO THROUGH COMPLETE METAMORPHOSIS. The four stages of complete metamorphosis are egg, larva, pupa, and adult. Each stage looks and behaves very differently.

skin. Then they can see and begin to eat. Their first meal may even be a weaker brother or sister. They also begin to chew on the wall of the egg sac. As they chew, their digestive juices help break down the sac walls. When a hole opens in it, the spiderlings crawl out.

Compare these nursery spiderlings to the adult. Besides being smaller and having shorter legs, they may have slightly different markings. Still, they can do anything adults can do except mate and produce young.

SPIDERLINGS

ADULT

Fishing spiders are also sometimes called nursery web spiders. That's because the females provide special care for their developing young. This care starts as soon as the eggs are laid.

After mating, this dark fishing spider spins a small silk mat. She deposits several hundred eggs on the silk. Next, she spins more silk, wrapping up her cluster of eggs. Then the female uses her chelicerae to pick up and hold onto the egg sac. For about three weeks, she carries it with her wherever she goes.

FISHING SPIDER FACT

The fishing spider's egg sac is about as big around as a U.S. nickel.

EGG SAC

Like all fishing spider females, this female fen raft fishing spider uses her silk to create a web around her egg sac. When the spiderlings leave the egg sac, they stay in the web for about a week. The female stays on the nursery web or nearby. She doesn't provide any food or additional care for her young. But she stays on guard against predators (hunters). Just by being there, she helps the young survive.

FISHING SPIDER FACT

Fishing spiderlings often cluster together in a ball in their nursery web. If they sense tiny movements in the web threads, they scatter in every direction. If the movements are caused by a predator, at least some spiderlings escape.

FISHING FOR A LIVING

The focus of a fishing spider's life is catching prey. Lots of other spiders are hunting prey too. Fishing spiders have found a place to hunt insect prey where most spiders are unable to go—on the surface of ponds, lakes, and slow-flowing rivers. They even reach underwater to snag tadpoles and little fish that come close.

Most fishing spiders, like this raft spider, hunt from a leaf raft or the shore. Their vision isn't very good, but that doesn't matter since they mostly hunt at night. And they mainly hunt by feel. They sit with several of their feet touching the water's surface. Some of the hairs on their legs are sensitive hairs, called trichobothria (trik-uh-BAWTH-ree-uh). These hairs pick up changes in air movement. Fishing spiders also have slit organs close to their leg joints. When ripples of water touch the spider's legs, the slit organs sense this. The spider can tell when the ripples are caused by something alive moving in the water. Which of the spider's legs move and how much they move lets the spider home in on prey in the water.

FISHING SPIDER FA[CT]

Fishing spiders can sense something moving as far away as 11 inches (30 centimeters).

If the ripples signal that what's moving is the size of prey, the fishing spider does something amazing. It walks and runs on water.

Water, like all matter, is made up of tiny building blocks, called molecules. The molecules at the surface of the water are strongly attracted to one another and to the water molecules below them. This makes the surface of the water act as if it has a thin skin. Scientists call this the water's surface tension.

A fishing spider's legs and abdomen have a dense coat of hair. Water can't get between these hairs. They repel water. This is what lets fishing spiders stay on top of the water's skinlike surface. Like all fishing spiders, this six-spotted fishing spider is able to push the ends of its legs into the water's surface without breaking the surface tension. The result is a small dimple in the water's surface.

Each time the great raft spider pulls its leg from front to back through the water it pushes the dimple formed by that leg. This acts like a rowboat's oar. The backward-moving dimple pushes the spider forward. Then the spider swings its leg forward through the air, pushes down on the water again, and again moves forward. The spider usually only rows with its middle two pairs of legs— one pair after the other. The front and rear pairs stay on the surface, keeping the spider steady. But even though it's only rowing with two pairs of legs, the spider covers about 1 foot (0.3 meter) per second. That's fast enough to catch a dragonfly struggling to escape the water's surface tension.

Fishing spiders use this same skill to escape predators. But most fishing spiders, like this dark fishing spider, move even faster to get away from danger. To put on speed, it straightens its legs to launch itself straight upward. When it lands on the water again, it pulls its front three pairs of legs—one pair after the other—through the water. This motion is almost like jumping through the water.

FISHING SPIDER FACT

A fishing spider can zip across the water's surface at about 3 feet (1 m) per second.

To escape flying predators, such as bats, fishing spiders dive underwater. As this fen raft spider dives, air is trapped between its body hairs. This layer of air, looking like a silver wet suit, coats the spider's body. The spider is able to breathe by drawing in oxygen from this air-filled coat. A gas naturally moves from where there's a lot of it to where there's less. Because of this, the oxygen (which is a gas) moves from the water into the spider's air-filled coat. This oxygen replaces the oxygen the spider uses as it breathes. While underwater, it can swim with the same leg motions it uses to row. But this movement uses up a lot of energy. So when escaping underwater, a fishing spider usually moves to a water plant and holds on. Later, it climbs back up to the surface.

FISHING SPIDER FACT

Fishing spiders can stay underwater for as long as thirty minutes.

FISH SOUP AND BUG JUICE

The sun is rising on a warm June day in England. A gentle breeze stirs ripples on the pond. But this female raft fishing spider isn't fooled by the waves. The slit organs on her legs pick up other water movements. They signal something prey sized is swimming just below the water surface and coming closer. Because the tiny ripple movements are stronger on one leg than another, she homes in on this movement. When she senses the prey is close, she darts out. The female's feet stab into the water's surface tension. As if she were running across the surface of a trampoline, she springs toward her target.

FISHING SPIDER FACT

Fishing spiders can't move their eyes the way people can. When they look at something, they have to turn their whole body toward it.

The raft fishing spider runs fast, pokes her legs below the surface, and snags a little fish. ZING! She jabs her fangs into the fish, injecting a dose of venom. She continues to hold on so her prey won't slip away in the water. Almost at once, the venom goes to work, and the fish stops moving. The fishing spider drags the fish up onto a leaf. There she jabs the fish yet again. This time, besides venom, the fishing spider injects some digestive juices into the little hole her fangs made. Within seconds, these juices turn the fish's soft tissues into a soup.

Like all spiders, the fishing spider has a very small mouth. She sucks up this fish soup. Hairs in her pharynx block hard bits. Only liquid can pass through into her stomach. Then the fishing spider throws up more digestive juices and repeats the process. When all that's left are bones and scaly skin, the spider lets go of this garbage. Then she begins hunting again.

Two days and several failed attempts later, she catches more prey. This time she feeds on a damselfly *(below)*. This prey gives her the energy boost she needs to continue to grow and develop.

Soon the female fishing spider's exoskeleton becomes too tight. She climbs up some plants growing at the pond's edge. Then she spins silk to anchor herself to a stalk. She spins a long silk line from the anchor silk and dangles from it. Her armorlike covering splits open, and the female spider crawls out *(facing page)*. Her body is already covered by a new exoskeleton.

This new exoskeleton is soft at first. The spider forces blood into different parts of her body to stretch the soft exoskeleton. This was her final molt. She now has adult parts and is ready to mate and produce young.

OLD EXOSKELETON

BECOMING PARENTS

This male raft fishing spider also recently molted to become an adult. He spins a tiny web, crawls over it, and deposits his sperm (male reproductive cells). He picks up the sperm from this web with his pedipalps and goes in search of a mate. To help him find her, the female gives off pheromones (FAIR-uh-mohnz). Pheromones are chemical signals. They help males find females. A male raft fishing spider will only mate with a female raft fishing spider.

FISHING SPIDER FACT

A female's pedipalps are shaped like little legs. A male's look as if he's wearing boxing gloves.

The male fishing spider slowly walks across the water toward the female. To signal he's a mate, not prey, he taps the water with his legs. She senses this unique pattern of ripples and stays still. When he's very close—close enough for her to see him—he stops. Then he slowly bobs his body up and down. Watching, she makes the same moves. He steps closer. She doesn't attack. Finally, the male darts in, inserts his sperm into her gonopore (reproductive opening), and hurries away.

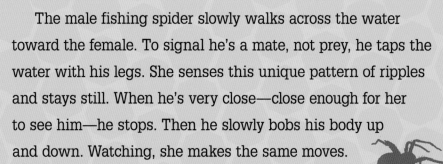

FISHING SPIDER FACT

Female fishing spiders can be up to 1 inch (2.6 cm) long. Their leg span can be as big as 3 inches (7.6 cm) across—nearly double the size of males. The females sometimes attack and eat courting males.

The female fishing spider keeps hunting for about a week. She needs plenty of food energy so her eggs will develop. Then she spins a silk disk. She deposits several hundred eggs one at a time on this disk. As each egg cell leaves her body through her gonopore, it passes the male's sperm stored in the spermatheca. When egg and sperm join, a baby spider starts to develop. A tough coating forms around each egg. After all the eggs are laid, the female fishing spider spins more silk. She wraps her whole batch of eggs in silk. It hardens into a tough egg sac. She picks this up with her chelicerae.

The female's egg sac is a big load to carry. It weighs nearly one-third as much as she does. Still, she carries the sac with her wherever she goes. Because she holds it with her mouthparts, she can't hunt while her babies are developing.

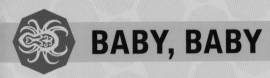

BABY, BABY

The fishing spider babies develop for about three weeks inside their egg sac. They receive the energy they need from the yolk (stored food) inside the egg. Even after the spiderlings hatch from their eggs, they stay inside their egg sac. They live off their bodies' stored food energy while they keep growing. After fishing spiderlings molt for the first time, they're ready to leave the egg sac.

When the female fishing spider senses her young are active, she climbs plants near the edge of the pond. She sticks the egg sac to a leaf with a bit of her silk. She spins more silk to create a tentlike web around the egg sac. Just as she finishes, the spiderlings chew an opening in the silk wall of the sac. Then they crawl out onto the web threads of their nursery.

The spiderlings still have enough stored food energy to grow a bit more. They'll be big enough to molt a second time before they leave the nursery web. Although she doesn't really do anything for her young, the female fishing spider is much bigger than her young are. She stays alert and on guard for predators, such as wasps. If a predator approaches, she attacks it to defend herself. This also keeps the spiderlings safe.

When the young leave, they go quickly. Once they're out of the nursery web, their mother is likely to eat any of them she can catch. The youngsters move into the pond and stay safe among the floating weeds. There they hunt and catch water insects even smaller than they are.

FISHING SPIDER FACT

If there are a lot of spiderlings in one area, some leave by ballooning. They shoot silk into the air and hang on. This silk is blown by the wind, and the spiderling is carried along.

THE CYCLE CONTINUES

As the days become cooler and fade more quickly into night, the female fishing spider mates again and raises a second batch of spiderlings. By then, many of the insects living in the pond begin to find shelters where they can rest for the winter. Running out of energy, the female raft fishing spider dies. Her body floats briefly on the pond that was her hunting grounds. A fish gulps it down. Meanwhile, one of her offspring, a little female fishing spiderling, crawls into the leaf litter at the pond's edge. There she finds a sheltered spot. Her body slows down so much she doesn't need to eat. This way, she can stay safe while cold winds blow, snow piles up on the leaf litter, and ice crusts over the pond.

When spring comes, the female fishing spiderling leaves her protected spot. So do the water striders, damselflies, and other insects she hunts on the pond. She continues to grow, molt, and grow some more. By the time she's an adult, she's even able to catch fish and tadpoles. This bigger prey gives her the energy she needs to mate and produce eggs. And a fishing spider's life cycle continues.

FISHING SPIDERS AND OTHER WATER ARACHNIDS

FISHING SPIDERS, or *Dolomedes,* belong to a group, or order, of arachnids called Araneae (ah-RAN-ee-ay). These are the spider members of the arachnid group. Fishing spiders belong to a family of spiders, the Pisauridae (pih-ZOHR-ee-dee) that build nursery webs. *Dolomedes* are a type of fishing spiders within this family. There are about one hundred different kinds of *Dolomedes* spiders worldwide.

SCIENTISTS GROUP living and extinct animals with others that are similar. So fishing spiders are classified this way:

kingdom: Animalia
phylum: Arthropoda
class: Arachnida
order: Araneae
family: Pisauridae

HELPFUL OR HARMFUL? Fishing spiders are helpful because they eat insects that spend at least part of their life cycle in water. This helps control insect populations, such as disease-carrying mosquitoes, that could otherwise become dangerous pests. Though the fishing spider's bite does inject venom, its venom isn't known to be harmful to people. Some people, though, may have an allergic reaction to any spider's bite.

HOW BIG IS a female six-spotted fishing spider? Its body is about 0.8 inches (2 cm) long.

OTHER WATER-LIVING ARACHNIDS

Only a few arachnids live and hunt mainly in water habitats. Compare the lives and hunting behavior of these two arachnids to the fishing spider.

Diving bell spiders are found in northern and central Europe and in Asia. This spider is the only one that spends every stage of its life underwater. Still, it breathes air like land-dwelling spiders. It's able to breathe underwater because it has a dense coat of short hairs covering its legs and abdomen. The coat traps air around its body. Both males and females spin silk sheets between branches of plants that grow underwater. Then they carry air bubbles down into the water and release the air under the silk sheets. They use these air chambers as retreats (safe places). Adults only occasionally have to bring fresh oxygen to this retreat. That's because oxygen naturally passes from the water (where there's a lot of it) through the silk and into the retreat's bubble (where there's less). This keeps the air supply steady.

Water mite adults are as tiny as a speck, only 0.11 inch (0.3 cm) long. The mites can be found swimming and crawling on the bottoms of ponds, marshes, and lakes worldwide. Mite larvae (babies) are parasites. They attach themselves to mosquito larvae, dragonfly larvae, or other insects that live in water. They suck the host's body juices. When the larvae have grown large enough to molt and become nymphs, they drop off their hosts. Water mite nymphs have eight legs and look like adults. They hunt and feed the way adults do.

GLOSSARY

abdomen: the rear end of an arachnid. It contains systems for digestion; reproduction; and, in spiders, silk production.

adult: the reproductive stage of an arachnid's life cycle

book lungs: thin, flat folds of tissue where blood circulates

brain: the organ that sends and receives messages from the rest of the body

caeca: branching tubes through which liquid food passes and where food is stored

cephalothorax: the front end of an arachnid. It includes the mouth, the brain, and the eyes. Legs are also attached to this part.

chelicerae: a pair of strong, jawlike parts that extend from the head in front of the mouth and end in fangs that can inject venom

coxal glands: special groups of cells for collecting and getting rid of liquid wastes through openings to the outside of the body. They aid in maintaining water balance in the body.

egg: a female reproductive cell; also the name given to the first stage of an arachnid's life cycle

exoskeleton: a protective, armorlike covering over the outside of the body

eyes: sensory organs that detect light and send signals to the brain for sight

fangs: a pair of toothlike parts on the spider's chelicerae. Venom flows out of the fangs through a hole near the tip.

gut: the body part where food nutrients pass into the blood to be carried throughout the body

heart: the muscular tube that pumps blood

Malpighian tubules: a system of tubes that cleans the blood of wastes

molt: the process of an arachnid shedding its exoskeleton

nerve ganglia: bundles of nerve tissue that send messages between the brain and other body parts

ovary: the body part that produces eggs

pedicel: the waistlike part in spiders that connects the cephalothorax to the abdomen

pedipalps: a pair of leglike body parts that extend from the head near the mouth. They help catch prey and hold it for eating. In males the pedipalps are also used during reproduction.

pharynx: a muscular body part that contracts to create a pumping force, drawing food into the body's digestive system. Hairs filter out any solid waste bits.

pheromones: chemicals given off as a form of communication

predator: an animal that catches and kills other animals, its prey, to survive

prey: animals caught by predators

regeneration: to regrow a lost body part

silk gland: the body part that produces silk

sperm: the male reproductive cell

spermatheca: a sac in female arachnids that stores sperm after mating

spiderling: the name given to the stage between egg and adult in spiders

spinneret: the body part that spins silk

spiracle: a small opening in the exoskeleton that leads into the trachea

stercoral pocket: the place where body wastes collect before passing out of the body

sucking stomach: a body part that along with the pharynx pulls liquid food into the arachnid's gut. Cells in the lining produce digestive juices.

tracheae: tubes that help spread oxygen throughout the spider's body. They also store oxygen.

venom: liquid poison

venom gland: the body part that produces venom

DIGGING DEEPER

To keep on investigating fishing spiders, explore these books and online sites.

BOOKS

Bishop, Nic. *Nic Bishop Spiders*. New York: Scholastic, 2007. This photo-rich book lets you compare fishing spiders to other kinds of spiders.

Cooper, Jason. *Fishing Spiders*. Vero Beach, FL: Rourke Publishing, 2006. Pictures and text help you discover more about these spiders.

Silverstein, Alvin, Virginia Silverstein, and Laura Silverstein Nunn. *Creepy Crawlies*. Minneapolis: Lerner Publications Company, 2003. Discover which arachnids and insects make good pets and which ones don't.

Singer, Marilyn. *Venom*. Minneapolis: Millbrook Press, 2007. Find out about creatures that can harm or even kill with a bite or a sting.

Souza, D. M. *Packed with Poison!* Minneapolis: Millbrook Press, 2006. Learn about the most venomous and poisonous animals in the world.

Townsend, John. *Incredible Arachnids*. Chicago: Heinemann-Raintree, 2005. See how fishing spiders are like other arachnids and how they are different.

MORE FROM SANDRA MARKLE

ARACHNID WORLD:
Black Widows
Harvestmen
Orb Weavers
Scorpions
Ticks
Wolf Spiders

WEBSITES

National Geographic: Fishing Spider Eats Frogs
http://www.youtube.com/watch?v=qNIF7aA3LgQ
Watch a spider catch and eat a frog.

Picsearch: Fishing Spiders
http://www.picsearch.com/pictures/animals/spiders/spiders%20a-f/
fishing%20spiders.html
This site offers lots of great photos of
fishing spiders. Click on any you'd like
to see enlarged.

University of Kentucky: Kentucky
Critter Files
http://www.uky.edu/Ag/CritterFiles/
casefile/spiders/fishing/pisaurid
Investigate fishing spiders that live in
the United States.

LERNER SOURCE™

Visit www.lerneresource.com
for free, downloadable arachnid
diagrams, research assignments
to use with this series, and
additional information about
arachnid scientific names.

FISHING SPIDER ACTIVITY

This investigation will let you discover how a fishing spider's air-filled coat helps it breathe underwater.

1. Fill a pie plate with water. Wait until the surface appears smooth. Try to lay a paper clip on the surface. It will immediately sink.

2. Rub petroleum-based jelly like Vaseline on a second paper clip. Place this paper clip on a piece of waxed paper while you wipe any excess jelly off your fingers.

3. Take the paper clip off the waxed paper, and hold the paper clip so its length is parallel to the surface of the water. Carefully lay the coated paper clip on the surface. The coating on the clip lets it float on the water's skinlike surface tension—just the way a fishing spider stands on water.

INDEX

PHOTO ACKNOWLEDGMENTS

The images in this book are used with the permission of: © Nicolas Petit/Bios/Photolibrary, p. 4; © Gary Meszaros/Photo Researchers, Inc., p. 5; © age fotostock/SuperStock, pp. 6–7; © Laura Westlund/Independent Picture Service, pp. 8–9; © Ross Nolly/NHPA/Photoshot, p. 11 (top); © Bryce McQuillan, p. 11 (bottom); © Gerry Bishop/Visuals Unlimited, Inc., p. 12; © Martyn F. Chillmaid/Photo Researchers, Inc., p. 13; © Alastair MacEwen/Oxford Scientific/Getty Images, pp. 14–15; © R. B. Suter, Vassar College, p. 17, 21; © Sinclair Stammers/naturepl.com, pp. 18–19, 33; © Science Faction/SuperStock, p. 23; © Geoff Dore/naturepl.com, pp. 24–25; © Oxford Scientific/Photolibrary, pp. 26–27, 41 (top); © Stephen Dalton/naturepl.com, pp. 28, 38–39; © Hans Pfletschinger/Peter Arnold Images/Photolibrary, p. 29; © Francesco Tomasinelli/Natural Visions, pp. 30, 37; © NHPA/SuperStock, p. 31; © Andy Newman/Woodfall Wild Images/NHPA/Photoshot, p. 32; © Reinhard Hölzl/imagebroker/Alamy, p. 35; © James H. Robinson/Photo Researchers, Inc., p. 41 (bottom); © Harry Rogers/Photo Researchers, Inc., p. 47.

Front cover: © Stephen Dalton/Minden Pictures.

Main body text set in Glypha LT Std 55 Roman 12/20. Typeface provided by Adobe Systems.